THE PROVI

AND

THE EXISTENCE OF EVIL

*A philosophical thesis
on the problem of evil*

Author:
Fr. Michael M. Gauvreau F.I.

ACADEMY OF THE IMMACULATE
NEW BEDFORD, MA
2004

The Providence of God and The Existence of Evil is a book prepared for publication by the Franciscans of the Immaculate [marymediatrix.com]. POB 3003, New Bedford, MA, 02741-3003.

Cum permissu superiorum
May 31, 2004
Feast of the Visitation of the Blessed Virgin Mary

DEDICATION

To my earthly mother who had the generosity to make the offering and to my heavenly mother, the Immaculate, who was willing to accept the offering.

To all those who were always prepared to give me an account for the hope that was in them and in turn motivating me to give reason for the hope that is in me. (cf. 1 Pet 3:15)

Finally, to those who sincerely seek the truth, may Our Lord God who, reveals these things to the merest of children and who has hidden them from those who are learned and wise (cf. Mt 11:25), bring you into the fullness of the truth under the mantle of Our Lady.

TABLE OF CONTENTS

THE PROVIDENCE OF GOD

AND

THE EXISTENCE OF EVIL

I
INTRODUCTION

"The foolishness of God is wiser than the wisdom of men"[1]

All men desire to know all things[2], but if there is one consistent in life it is that no man actually knows all things. This is most apparent when one is faced with two realities, namely, God and evil, which seem to be in such contradiction; Given the existence of an all-powerful, all-knowing, and all-good God, how can there be evil, and how can it be reconciled with this same God's goodness, power and knowledge?

---

[1] 1 COR 1:25

[2] ARISTOTLE, *Metaphysica* 1.1, 980, a2, 1

Many philosophies[3] have arisen in response to this so-called "dilemma", which either attempt to suggest solutions to the problem, or ignore it all together. One attempted solution is to deny outright God's existence. Another is to deny effectively His existence, by denying one or more of His attributes, by statements such as these: "God must not be all-good"; "God can't be all-powerful and all-knowing, for if he is, there should be no evil, pain or suffering". At the other extreme, some even deny the existence of evil. These statements are attempts to avoid contradiction, by arbitrarily redefining different aspects of the two realities which are involved.

When confronted by his intellectual limitations and ignorance of the answer to a given question, man will, predictably, invent an answer anyway, which usually means sacrificing the truth in order to satisfy the desire for an answer, whether sincere or not. Listen to an inquisitive child asking his father basic questions of life. Until the ultimate one comes up, "How did everything get here?"

---

[3] See Glossary

Or, "If God made everything, who made God? And if nobody made God how did He get here? Obviously, not many children receive immediate and satisfactory answers to these questions. Perhaps they are told to "stop asking silly questions", or that there are no answers.   The parent, who attempts to answer seriously without being sure of the correct answer, will be backed into a corner by the little metaphysician[4] creating a bigger problem than there was previously.

In dealing with the topic of God's Providence and the existence of evil, we must take these two, as they are, namely, realities; the fact of Divine Providence and the fact of evil. In trying to understand the two, we must try also to see the relation between them. This booklet is intended for those who are inquisitive, in the manner of a child who seeks to understand a certain aspect of reality that he knows is a fact, but who admits readily he doesn't "get it", as they say, and seeks his solutions from those who might. This booklet borrows from the traditional, perennial knowledge

---

[4] See Glossary

and wisdom of the scholastics[5], which, while asserting the Benevolence of God and the existence of evil, nevertheless finds in this nothing so irreconcilable, according to right reason, that a solution cannot be had by sincere seekers of the truth.

In a subject of this nature, there are two parallel objectives: one of exposition, and one of argumentation, defense or explanation. For those who would like to understand what they believe, a sufficient exposition of the concepts involved will be all that is necessary. But for those who, because of difficulties, have a wrong concept of God, or disbelieve all together, a defense must be given. Not that this presentation will be satisfactory for all, because no matter how well the exposition or the defense of a position, there will always be those who will have difficulties and doubts, especially when the truth is demanding.

---

[5] Any student of medieval philosophy favoring argumentation and discussion through a systematic use of logic. St. Thomas Aquinas and St. Bonaventure, philosophers of the thirteenth century are often identified with scholastic thought.

We then move from a problem of the intellect, to that of the will. As Bishop Fulton Sheen once said, "For those who believe, no proof is necessary, but for those who do not, no proof is enough."

II
THE EXISTENCE OF
PROVIDENCE

The idea of some kind of Divine Providence, however obscure, exists among most men, yet there are always some, who deny any kind of Divine Providence. Further along in the chapter I will try to explain how this denial is in some way a type of intellectual suicide because it leads to anarchy, rebellion and also opens the door to Tyranny.

Man strives to be the sole governor of his destiny and claims for himself a divine right, precisely as a rationalization of a tyrannical self-will. This was the error of the many tyrannical dictators of the past century and this was the error that St. Francis of Assisi wanted far removed from his friars who were always to be minors, the least of the brethren, humble and submissive to their superiors. He used very strong language and described this tendency to exalt private judgment and glorify individualistic self-will as vomit, that is the basest thing there is.

Ruling the world can only be achieved by a being that is all-wise, all-good and all-powerful or it is bound to fail.

The crux of the matter is such, that anyone who promotes a philosophy claiming any authenticity or credibility must provide a credible explanation of common sense experience. This means facing the most evident fact observable in reality; the obvious order, harmony and purpose which pervades the cosmos, as a whole, to the smallest part of the universe, discovered in the cloister of the atom. (Which we have discovered isn't so cloistered after all).

William Paley (1743-1805) theologian, philosopher and scientist, used the analogy of someone discovering a watch while walking on a beach, and concluding that there must be a watchmaker. If this is so how much more does the universe require an intelligent designer?[6] Following this line of thought, if one were to place into a bag all the pieces that it takes to make a watch, how many times would one have to shake the bag, before all the parts came together to make a watch, just by chance?

The Order, harmony and purpose of the universe cannot be derived from chaos. Chaos cannot order, it cannot plan, and is inherently incapable of bringing forth from itself something which it does not have, namely, an order and purpose evidenced in the things of nature, beautifully moving to their proper ends. Nature cannot reflect on itself; it cannot give reason for

---

[6] PALEY, WILLIAM, In *Dictionary of Philosophy and Religion,* W.L Reese, Humanities Press, New Jersey, 1980 cf. Similar considerations can be found in the recent critique of evolution from the standpoint of final causality by MICHAEL BEHE, *Darwin's Black Box,* The Free Press, New York, 1996 and MICHAEL BEHE, *Science & Evidence for Design in the Universe,* San Francisco, 2002

its existence or for its action, determined by invisible forces, which scientists have classified under the physical laws of nature.

As it is said, "It takes one to know one"; whether you are looking in through a microscope or out through a telescope, it is clear that you are faced with a well ordered plan, coming from an Intellect far greater than the one you possess. This well-ordered plan is attributed to God as its origin and end, under the direction of His Divine Providence.

"In the consideration of this subject, one thing impressed itself upon my mind with constantly increasing emphasis. It was the absolute impossibility of believing, that, in this limitless expanse of flaming suns and countless constellations, *no one understands its origin and mysteries more than we do;* and that our feeble, finite intellects form the highest limit of intelligence existing in this wondrous scheme of things!

That thought is ridiculous in its conceit, and paralyzing in its influence. We may talk academically of a "Godless world," but when we really face its possibility, we find that there is nothing more appalling in its horror than the conception of a boundless universe, eternally evolving in perfect order and in full activity...*without a Mind to comprehend, or Will to guide it!* "Man," says Disraeli, "is made to adore and to obey." When we conceitedly survey our puny selves, we fain would disbelieve this statement; but when we look off from our darkened planet into starlit space, we know that it is true."[7]

---

[7] JOHN L. STODDARD, *Rebuilding a Lost Faith,* Tan, Illinois, 1990, Pg.56

III
CONCEPT OF PROVIDENCE AND GOVERNMENT

The word providence comes from the Latin "*providere*", which means, "to look ahead", implying or signifying a certain "care for". Applied to man, providence comes under the cardinal virtue of prudence. Thus, one is wise and providential, who fittingly orders to the end of life those who are subject to him.

"This is evident in an army: all divisions of an army and their functions are ordered to the commander's good as an ultimate end, and this is victory. And for this reason it is the function of the commander to govern the whole army. Likewise, an art which is concerned with the end commands and makes the laws for an art concerned with means to the end. Thus, the art of civil government commands that of the military; the military commands the equestrian; and the art of navigation commands that of shipbuilding."[8]

Thomas Aquinas also uses the example of a father providing for his family, or a King who, for the good of his kingdom, must order or rule wisely those subject to him[9].　Providence consequently involves someone who has a plan, *a priori[10]*, which his subjects must follow to reach their end, and who has sufficient and adequate means or power to execute this plan, called governance.

"A prudent person will first desire the end and then, having decided on the

---

[8] St. Thomas, *Summa Contra Gentiles, Providence,* Bk. 3, Part 1, Ch. 64

[9] St. Thomas, *Summa Theologica* part 1, Q.22, Art.1

[10] See Glossary

means to be employed, will begin using them; thus the end, which held first place in his desire, is the last in actual attainment. So we look upon God as intending from all eternity first the end and purpose of the universe and then the means necessary for the realization or attainment of that end. This commonsense view is expressed by the philosophers when they say that the end is first in the order of intention but the last in order of execution."[11]

The philosophers referred to by Rev. Garriguo-Lagrange are the scholastics mentioned in chapter one and also Aristotle from whom St. Albert the Great and St. Thomas Aquinas received much of their philosophical foundations.

The principle, "The end is the first in the order of execution," expressed in the paragraph quoted above can be clarified if we try to

---

[11] REV. REGINALD GARRIGUO-LAGRANGE, O.P., *Providence,* Herder, St. Louis, 1937, Pg.158

understand that before the completion of any project or human endeavor such as constructing a building or something as mundane as making a cup of coffee the intention or desire for each of these things must be first and the actual possession of the thing must come last. Meaning that the end, viz., the building or the coffee is desired first or is first in the order of intention-in the mind but in reality its actual attainment or execution is last.

By this understanding we see what is properly fitting to God in the governance of creation as St. Thomas teaches;

"I answer that, it is necessary to attribute providence to God. For all the good that is in created things has been created by God, as was shown above (Q. 6, A. 4). In created things good is found not only as regards their substance, but also as regards their order towards an end and especially their last end, which, as was said above, is the divine goodness (Q. 21,

A. 4). This good of order existing in things created, is itself created by God. Since, however, God is the cause of things by His intellect, and thus it behooves that the type of every effect should pre-exist in Him, as is clear from what has gone before (Q. 19, A. 4), it is necessary that the type of the order of things towards their end should pre-exist in the divine mind: and the type of things ordered towards an end is, properly speaking, providence."[12] (This quotation is hard to understand but I will explain it afterwards)

A created intellectual nature, *viz.*, man, in its providence can only plan and execute according to its knowledge and power, which is always limited, no matter how exalted. It has no control over every cause outside its knowledge, and thus, the providence exercised is always contingent, and to a certain degree, imperfect and fallible.

---

[12] St. Thomas Aquinas, *Summa Theologica,* Christian Classics, Texas, 1948, vol. 1, Part 1, Q. 22, Art. 1

Providence is attributed to God properly speaking because nothing falls outside His knowledge and Power, and as such, His plan and its execution is perfect and infallible, in accordance with the end which He wills.

> "Concerning God's wisdom, the following must be held. This wisdom most clearly knows all things, good and evil, past, present, and future, actual and possible. Thus it also knows things beyond our understanding and things eternal; in its awareness of all that is to come about, it is called prescience or foresight; in its awareness of what God Himself will do, it is called providence."[13]

From what was stated above, we can compare God's plan and its execution to the architect's blueprint and the resulting construction according to it. God's plan is what is referred to in the proper sense by the term "providence". This is

---

[13] St. Bonaventure, *Breviloquium,* Part 1, Ch. 8, N. 1

the Eternal art of God, the exemplars[14], and the idea existing in the Divine Mind of the order of creatures to their ends.

> "Not only does this wisdom imply the power of knowing: it actually is the very principle of knowing all that is known; it is called **exemplar** as being the principle of all that is foreseen and disposed also in respect to things as they proceed from God, He is the Exemplar. To the exemplar pertain **idea**, **word**, **art**, and **purpose**: *Idea,* as regards the act of foreseeing; *word,* as regards the act of proposing; *art,* as regards the act of carrying out; and *purpose,* as regards the act of completing, for it adds final intention."[15]

When we speak executively of Divine Providence, we are concerned with the guidance and governance of what God has made according

---

[14] See Glossary

[15] St. Bonaventure, *Breviloquium,* Part 1, Ch.8, N. 2

to that Eternal plan in His mind. In accord with this plan, the Divine Will freely calls creatures into being and directs them to their proper ends, according to their natures whether free or determined[16]. Divine Providence is thus both eternal and temporal, the former, in plan, the latter as execution of the plan, carried out in time and destined to cease when everything is completed. Providence presupposes Goodness in fittingly directing things for the good of the whole creation.

As it was stated in the previous paragraph that God creates for a purpose so that after He brings a thing into being He also concerns himself with the attainment of that creature's purpose, completion, fulfillment or end. The end of a creature is nothing less than the attainment of the purpose for which it was made. The end or purpose, for example, of prayer is union with God and when this union is attained, prayer has achieved its goal or end. The answer to the question of why a thing exists is found in its purpose or end; so to the question of why someone

---

[16] St. Bonaventure, *Breviloquium,* Part.1, Ch.8, N. 6

studies we say in order to understand because understanding is the purpose or end of study. This is of utmost importance when we desire to know and attain our end or the purpose for which we exist- to know, love, and serve God in this life so that we may be happy with Him in the next.

IV
DIFFICULTIES WITH PROVIDENCE AND IT'S RELATION TO EVIL

A question difficult to answer, is raised by some, who, while admitting that there is obviously some sort of providence in the world, and an order of good, cannot attribute it to our concept of God because of the existence of evil in the world. The question is posed in this manner: *"how, given the fact of an all-powerful and all-good God, from whose providence nothing escapes, can there be so much evil in the world?"* Either there is no God at all, or God isn't all-powerful, which explains why He cannot do anything about evil; or isn't all-good, and doesn't really care one way or the other.

Atheism[17]

The easiest solution is to deny the existence of God because of the existence of evil, but this is to oversimplify things. For their remains, on the one hand, that still unexplained fact of evil, and on the other that unexplained or unaccounted for good. Atheism is like an ostrich that buries its head in the sand on the assumption that, "If I can't see you, you can't see me." It's illogical to deny every fact that points to God and His Providence, (not to mention dishonest.) It's like fixing a nosebleed by cutting off the head[18]. Those who choose this path are a minority, but when they do, the results are tragic.

Getting rid of God leaves the solution of the problem of evil up to man's own ingenuity and providence, and since no one likes evil, it's natural to try and eliminate it by setting up a plan directed to a natural state of happiness. It's been tried in the social system called Communism[19], a forced

---

[17] See Glossary

[18] SCOTT HAHN, Tape Series, *Where is God in an ungodly world?* tp#1, St. Joeseph's Communications

[19] See Glossary

and imposed happiness by means of tyranny. Atheists work towards this utopian society on the principle, "In order to make an omelet, you have to break a few eggs[20]", unconcerned that the eggs to be broken are human beings, not real eggs, and ignoring that this so-called necessary evil or process to happiness is what they attributed to Theism. The very basis on which they deny God's existence is the fact of evil in the world yet in their own system not only is evil not eliminated, it increases. Atheism itself uses all the proofs we need to junk the system. It is illogical and impractical. It does not solve the problem of evil, but instead takes away that only defense against evil we have; hope, and replaces it with despair.

Dualism[21]

Another, ever popular solution is that of *dualistic philosophy*, which sees no need to deny God's existence to explain the problem of evil, but which eliminates the omnipotence of God

---

[20] PETER KREEFT, *The problem of suffering,* Ann Arbor Michigan, 1986

[21] See Glossary

by proposing two ultimate principles of being. God is the ultimate principle of good, and is seen in spiritual natures, and the other is the principle of evil, and is the explanation for material existence. The two principles are in contradiction and war against each other. This is shown best in man, who is partly spirit and partly matter, and so in disorder, with the flesh lusting against the spirit. Contrary to this dualistic philosophy, it is certain that there cannot be two ultimate principles as the equal causes of all things, so that both principles are unique and really distinct from each other. This would imply that each possesses something the other has not, and each, therefore, be imperfect. The result is that since neither is perfect, neither could be an ultimate principle, for an ultimate principle must be in itself undivided, self-subsistent, and perfect, lacking nothing and requiring nothing for the perfection of its being.

Thus, we cannot, without contradiction, hold that two ultimate principles of any kind can account for everything that is. The theory as expressed here is that of the Manicheans[22]. It reappears in one way or another in the teaching of the medieval Albigensians and Cathari[23], opposed by Sts. Dominic and Anthony of Padua. It is found later in various forms of Protestantism (The Puritans are a good example with their constant association of material things with evil, viz., alcohol, cigarettes, etc....) and Jansenism[24]. More recently it is seen in literature and movies that portray life as a great drama between the ultimate principle of good and evil (Star Wars) and many eastern religions represented by the Chinese yin-yang symbol. They will be more clearly understood after adequately studying the nature of evil.

Deism and Pantheism[25]

Another attempted solution widespread today, is to claim existence of a God and His total power but to deny His goodness. That is the

---

[22] See Glossary

[23] See Glossary

[24] See Glossary

[25] See Glossary

problem; Ultimate power corrupts, right? So, God is all-powerful, and He creates only to torture and play the part of cruel scientist towards a laboratory rat, or even a cat, who toys with a mouse until it's dead. The problem is both the denial that God is all-good, and the claim that He is either a tyrant, or indifferent to the evil suffered in His creation. Two main philosophical proponents of this theory are *Deists* and *Pantheists*.

Deists hold that God, after creating, left the world to itself and does not bother with it anymore, like a watchmaker who makes a watch, winds it up, and leaves it to itself. Deists hold God's transcendence, (that attribute of God by which he is said to have an existence in an order and manner above and beyond all other things - His surpassing excellence) but deny his omnipresence in creation, *so misrepresenting His transcendence.*

Pantheism is the philosophy that does not deny God's goodness in the same way as Deism, nor does it deny God's power, as the Manichees.

It denies God's goodness indirectly, by combining all existence into a great blob. Thus, it eliminates God's transcendence and makes God just a part of the whole, being only immanent. In the pantheistic sense it describes God as present in and operating in the universe, but identifying him with the universe, *so misrepresenting His omnipresence.* God is good, but He has a dark side: He is both good and evil.

Pantheism holds to a reality that allows for no distinctions, and claims any apparent distinctions are only illusory, for everything is one and the same. I am God and you are God. It is attractive to those who wish to eliminate moral standards and to rid society of distinctions, such as the difference between man and woman, as many forms of *feminism*[26] do either explicitly or implicitly. It goes against the very foundations of thought; the principle of non-contradiction and identity that as a law of being and thought states that a thing cannot *be* and *not be* at the same time in the same respect. For example one can imagine

---

[26] See Glossary

a circle and a square as distinct objects both in the mind and verifiable in reality, yet one could never imagine nor find in reality a circle-square, its an impossible concept a contradiction.

Any system that denies the principle of non-contradiction obviously, as written above, goes against the foundation of thought. This is the case with the denial of fundamental differences between the concepts of man and woman. What is the reason? Because the attempt is made at denying the opposition between absolute concepts that cannot simultaneously both *be* or both *not be* in the same being.

Idealism (Christian Science)[27]

In the systems of philosophy just reviewed, the existence of God is denied or His attributes are misrepresented. If that is hard to fathom and harder to hold, what can be said of a system of philosophy which denies the existence of evil, when to our senses and general experience, it is the one of the facts most apparent to us. *Christian*

---

[27] See Glossary

Science, which is neither Christian nor scientific, holds that evil does not exist. The guru of this sophistry was Mary Baker Eddy, who held that evil is just an illusion. This is a form of *idealism*.

G.K. Chesterton said that the great problem of philosophy is why little Tommy loves to torture the cat. Idealism's solution is to deny the suffering of the cat[28]. Evil is all in the head and purely subjective in origin, a projection into reality, of that which isn't there. This is absurd; One thing determines the falsity of Christian Science; ***death***, too harsh and definite to be an illusion. If evil is an illusion, the illusion still needs to be accounted for.

"The primary principle of the cult obviously forbade them to run for a doctor if Mrs. Eddy broke her leg, since either the leg, or certainly the break, or possibly both, were illusions of mortal mind. Whether there really were people

---

[28] G. K. CHESTERTON, *Orthodoxy*, ch.2, pg.15, Image Books, New York, 1959

who would have let a man bleed to death, because the blood was a result of the mere flow of his thoughts, I have my doubts…[29]"

The systems of philosophy briefly sketched above are bankrupt, giving no tangible solution to the problem of evil. It could be objected that if these systems are so obviously empty and incomplete, at best, then why have so many great thinkers with capable native intelligence embraced them?

St. Thomas gives one answer, "To us, because we do not know for what reason divine providence arranges each event, it may seem that all things happen with equal indifference to the good and the wicked. Still there is no doubt that in all the good or evil that happens whither to the good or to the wicked there is a just design according to which divine providence disposes all. But because we do not know this, it seems to us that things

---

[29] G.K. CHESTERTON, Oct.18, 1930, In Illustrated London News, Collected Writings, San Francisco, 1991.

come to pass haphazardly and irrationally."[30]

We do not deny the native genius of these people, but we must realize that genius is not the measure of truth rather it deals with one's intellectual ability to learn and understand the truth. Even a genius can be very confused because of having no sound metaphysics or has never been presented with anything other than misconceptions of the truth.

Then at times the problem lies not in the head but in the heart because the truth in question requires a definite standard of living. Man is not all intellect but also has a will. In fact, most of the time, it is not intellectual knowledge that leads the will, but the will that leads the intellect. I know that smoking cigarettes is harmful for me, but I can still choose to smoke and even try reason against reason to justify my choice. The problem for these who possess genius lies not in the head but in the heart.

---

[30] St. Thomas Aquinas, *QQ. Disp. De Veritate, q. 5, a. 5,* In *Scholastic Metaphysics*, John F. McCormick S.J., Loyola Press, Illinois, 1943

"No doubt, some men are atheists for moral reasons. They wish to salve their consciences for they live as if there were no God. Often they are vociferous about their atheism like small boys who whistle in the dark to conceal their fears. Others are troubled by the common objections against the existence of God. Sometimes all they have heard about God are these objections. And to a man who does not think about them they may seem quite unanswerable. As Belloc says:

'Those who have replied and do reply "No God", have the immediate certitudes in their favor. One might draw a comparison here between the man who affirms that the earth is flat, against the man who affirms that the earth is round. The first man, who says it is flat, has on the face of it a solid case, and a case apparently more agreeable to the most immediate evidence than the second. The earth certainly seems flat as we go about on it.'

In the same way *there* seems at first sight to be no God, so far as the reason is concerned."[31]

---

[31] JOSEPH H. CAVANAUGH, C.S.C, *Evidence For Our Faith,* Notre Dame Press, Indiana, 1952, P.30

V
EVIL ACCORDING TO SCHOLASTIC PHILOSOPHY[32]

Now we turn to a system of philosophy which has stood the test of time, and so earned the title 'Perennial'. It is found in the greatest thinkers in history, who not only sought for the truth in mind, but also embraced it with their hearts. Their lives were dedicated to the pursuit of wisdom, and testified to it with their moral integrity. They merit a place in any discussion of philosophy, and carry much weight in their interpretation of reality, especially concerning the problem of evil and its relation to the Providence of God. Their authority is an indispensable support and encouragement for those wrestling to formulate an understanding of and solution to the problem.

---

[32] See Glossary

It's Concept in General

There can be no doubt that the presence of evil, which has baffled so many thinkers since the days of the Gnostics and Manichaeans, is not trivial and in truth is one of the most serious problems in philosophy that demands our attention. In fact, "Cardinal Newman considered it the greatest and the most perplexing of all problems. Nevertheless, we are able to solve this problem at least to the extent of seeing that the presence of evil in the world is not opposed to the wisdom and goodness of God."[33]

That evil exists is one of the easiest things to prove, because it surrounds us in daily life. When we speak of God being known through creation, we observe that such knowledge is possible, but only upon adequate reflection.   Evil, on the contrary, is discovered with little reflection. Evil in its most general sense can be found in an uncomfortable mosquito bite received, blindness in a man, injuries, the struggle for survival seen

---

[33] Austin G. Schmidt S. J., Joseph A. Perkins A.M., *Faith and Reason,* Loyola Press, Illinois, 1943

in the animal kingdom, suffering and death of millions through war, sickness and human cruelty. These are evils in various degrees, and one can continue enumerating specific evils indefinitely, and still not come to any concrete answer to the questions, "What is evil?   What is its nature?" The answer given by St. Augustine, and expounded by scholastics such as St. Bonaventure and St. Thomas Aquinas, tells us that we must not attribute to evil what is not proper to it, namely a nature or substantial existence of its own. Evil has no existence in itself, for it is merely a privation of good in some being, and not a positive being. Evil is an absence, a defect, a negation, a privation.

Evil is a lack of something in a good which is proper to it and which it ought to possess.

"For what is that which we call evil but the absence of good? In the bodies of animals, disease and wounds mean nothing but the absence of health; for when a cure is effected, that does not mean that the evils which were present-namely, the diseases and wounds-go away from the body and dwell elsewhere: they altogether cease to exist; for the wound or disease is not a substance, but a defect in the fleshly substance-the flesh itself being a substance, and therefore something good, of which those evils-that is, privations of the good which we call health-are accidents. Just in the same way, what are called vices in the soul are nothing but privations of natural good. And when they are cured, they are not transferred elsewhere: when they cease to exist in the healthy soul, they cannot exist anywhere else".[34]

We say darkness is only privation or the absence of light; or that blindness in an animal is the absence of sight; or sickness, the absence of health. Each example given: light, sight, and health, participate in being, having specific

---

[34] St. Augustine, *Enchridion; Faith, Hope, and Charity* Gateway Editions, Washington D.C, 1992 Ch.11, p.11

natures, and are therefore good in themselves. But the evils predicated of them: darkness, blindness, and sickness, are nothing in themselves. They have no nature, they exist only as the absence or privation of what ought to be present in a certain nature. If I lose my arm in some accident, it is an evil that no one would deny. But, why is it evil? It is evil because I ought to have an arm attached to my body. The accident is not evil, but the privation caused by the accident is evil.

Not everything that is a mere negation is an evil, e.g., when hands are negated of a bird, and when wings are negated of a man. These privations are not evils, for a bird ought not to have hands, and man ought not to have wings[35]. "In fact, evil is simply a privation of something which *a subject is entitled by its origin to possess and which it ought to have*, as we have said. Such is the meaning of the word "evil" among all men. Now, privation is not an essence; it is, rather, a negation in a substance."[36]

---

[35] ST. THOMAS, *Summa Contra Gentiles,* Bk3,Ch.6, Ch.7, Par.2

[36] ST. THOMAS, *Summa Contra Gentiles,* Bk3, Ch.7

Evil's Existence, Relation to God, and Origin

Though evil, a non-being, is not a positive reality, this isn't to say that evil does not exist as taught Christian Science. For it does exist in relation to good. On the other hand, of itself, contrary to the manichees, there can never be an ultimate principle of evil 'existing, *per se*'[37] as an ultimate principle of good can exist, '*per se*'. Evil is such by nature, that it requires a good being to exist in. Destroy the good, and the evil ceases to be, much like the hole in a donut ceases to exist after the donut has been eaten.

"Accordingly, there is nothing of what we call evil, if there be nothing good. But a good which is wholly without evil is a perfect good. A good, on the other hand, which contains evil is a faulty or imperfect good; and there can be no evil where there is no good. From all this we arrive at the curious result: that since every being, so far as it is a being, is good, when

---

[37] See Glossary

we say that a faulty being is an evil being, we just seem to say that what is good is evil, and that nothing but what is good can be evil, seeing that every being is good, and that no evil can exist except in a being. Nothing, then, can be evil except something which is good. And although this, when stated, seems to be a contradiction, yet the strictness of reasoning leaves us no escape from the conclusion."[38]

Contrariwise, to destroy the evil, is to perfect the good in which the evil, as privation, existed, by restoring that which is proper to it, and that which it ought to have, such as restoring health to a sick man, or sight to a blind man.

By regarding evil as it properly exists in relation to the good, we understand more clearly why God cannot in any way be evil Himself, and how as Creator, He cannot directly be the cause

[38] St. Augustine, *The Enchiridion on Faith, Hope, and Love,* Gateway, Washington, D.C., 1992

of evil in any way because God creates all things good.

That evil can have no part in God, is known from the manner in which He exists, as existence itself, 'pure act', and the supreme subsistent being[39]; in catechetical terms this means He is uncreated, always was, is and will be.

God as the *first* cause, the *unmoved* mover, is therefore in no way potentially anything else, which would imply an imperfection in God until he become or acquire that something else. For, "anything that is moved to become more perfect is moved by another; *Omne quod movetur ab alio movetur.*" God cannot become more perfect for He is all-perfect, He lacks nothing in His being.

To deny a being greater than which none other can be thought of and who is therefore in no way moved by another, thereby always

---

[39] ST. BONAVENTURE, *Breviloquium* Part.3, Ch.1, p.109; St.Thomas, *Summa Theologica*; Part 1, Q.4, Art.2, *"I answer..."*

possessing His own existence *a se* (from himself and not dependently from another), and being the source and cause of all other existence, is to posit an infinite degree of cause and effect, as such, untenable because unintelligible.

If a scientist proposes the theory of an infinitely expanding universe, he cannot evade such questions as, "A universe expanding from what, and into what is it expanding?" If it is expanding into something, then doesn't that something deserve to be included in what we call the universe?" It cannot be expanding into *nothing*, for *nothing* does not exist, and something can cease to exist, but cannot expand into non-existence.

One can imagine the outer limits of the universe (if there is such a thing imaginable, for if one could imagine a limit as a definite boundary one could also imagine by what it is limited), creating for itself space into which to expand, much like a train creating for itself the track onto which it moves along its continued course. As for an infinitely expanding universe, without limits arising from dependence on a first cause, a point of origin, this is equally untenable. So let's posit a "big bang". But, is that all there is to be said? If so, the big-bang is not a cause, for it still begs the question; where did the big bang come from?

> "The evolutionary materialists are appropriately enough represented in the vision of all things coming from an egg, a dim and monstrous oval germ that got laid itself by accident."[40]

All this shows that God is self-subsistent being, and as such, lacks no perfection in ultimate goodness, and in that goodness, no privation exists, therefore no such thing as evil[41].

God can no more be the cause of evil, *per se* than there could be evil in him, but He can be the cause of evil *indirectly*, as will be shown

---

[40] G.K CHESTERTON, *What's wrong with the world* Sheed & Ward, New York, 1956, Ch.2 p.7

[41] ST. BONAVENTURE, *Breviloquium.* Part.3, Ch.10, par.4, p.56
ST. THOMAS, *Summa Theologica* Part.1, Q.4, Art.1

below[42].

> "Just as the sun in the heavens gives light, whilst the shadow on the ground, the absence of light, is caused by the intervention of some obstacle, such as a tree, blocking out the rays of light; so the Infinitely Good God is the cause of nothing but goodness, the absence of goodness, wherever it occurs, being caused by the intervention of some creative object, not infrequently by the misuse of free will on the part of man."[43]

Distinguishing Types of Evil; Metaphysical, Physical and Moral

Metaphysical Evil

God is the Supreme Good from whom all things derive their existence. To some extent, all

---

[42] St. Thomas, *Summa Contra Gentiles* Ch.10, par.4, p.56

[43] Rev. Bertrand L. Conway, C.S.P., *The Question Box*, Paulist Press, New York, 1929

things participate in His Goodness, *for existence is the first good of any creature.* However, not all things participate in existence to the same degree. That is why there is a hierarchy of being. Being participates in Goodness to the degree in which it participates essentially in existence.

God is cause of all being, *per se,* and all being is good, *per se,* but unequal in its participation in His goodness. It is in the fundamental difference of each created nature that we say some evil necessarily exists. The technical and traditional term used to describe this unequal participation in goodness is *Metaphysical evil.* We call this evil only in an analogous sense because that which is apparently a disorder of nature is really no disorder, since it is part of a definite plan intended by the Creator. *Metaphysical evil* therefore, is an improper use of the term evil because it implies *imperfection*, when it should rather be understood as *relative perfection* in nature.

"But it is ridiculous to condemn the faults of beasts and trees, and other such mortal and mutable things as are void of intelligence, sensation, or life, even though these faults should destroy their corruptible nature; for these creatures received, at their Creator's will, an existence fitting them, by passing away and giving place to others, to secure that lowest form of beauty, the beauty of seasons, which in its own place is a requisite part of this world. For things earthly were neither to be made equal to things heavenly, nor were they, though inferior, to be quite omitted from the universe. Since, then, in those situations where such things are appropriate, some perish to make way for others that are born in their room, and the less succumb to the greater, and the things that are overcome are transformed into the quality of those that have the mastery, this is the appointed order of things transitory. Of this order the beauty does not strike us, because by our mortal frailty we are so involved in a part of it, that we cannot perceive the whole, in which these fragments that offend us are harmonized with the most accurate fitness and beauty. And therefore, where we are not so well able to perceive the wisdom of the Creator, we are very properly enjoined to believe it, lest in the vanity of human rashness we presume to find any fault with the work of so great an Artificer."[44]

If we are to have the splendor of the universe before our eyes and minds, in order to know something of the omnipotence and fullness of an infinite God, then the presence of some evil should not come as a surprise or shock, it is only the fact of moral evil or sin that is "shocking".

To deal with such "shock" therefore, we must distinguish between the two different orders of evil; the first is *physical evil,* and the second is *moral evil.*

---

[44] St. Augustine, *The City of God,* Random House, New York, 1950, Bk.12, N.4

Physical Evil

Physical evil is that which results from the conflict between creatures acting according to their specific natures. Examples are death, pain, and sickness. The world in which we live cannot avoid these evils. They are bound up in the good of the universe. A lion, to be a lion, must eat other animals, and consequently this means a loss, or evil, in the animal eaten—the privation of that animal's life. Privations of this kind pervade the animal and plant kingdoms. The loss of one being's life is the source of another's continuation of life[45].

Augmentation and reproduction are the perfection of vegetative life, yet nature seems to oppose both in storms, change of seasons, and animals' consumption. In a world of sentient creatures, pain and suffering are inevitable. To take each instance, as an example apart from the whole and lament over the tragic evils existing in the world, is somewhat narrow minded.

---

[45] St. Thomas, *Summa Theologica* Part.1, Q.48, Art.2&3

"As physical evil is opposed only to some finite good, it may, according to the right order, in a complicated system, where parts are subordinated to other parts and to the whole, be intended as a means to the well being of a higher order or of the whole. And hence, what may be considered a physical evil, if we confine our attention to one small portion of this complicated world-order, will be seen to be good if we consider that portion in its relation to others and to the whole. So, the loss of an arm, looked at merely in itself is a physical evil, but to lose an arm to save the whole man, is according to right order, and therefore, under that aspect, not an evil. So, sickness, which sends a man back to God, is not, if viewed adequately, an evil. God, therefore, may intend, if He wishes, the happening of physical evil as a means to a good in a higher order."[46]

---

[46] WILLIAM J. BROSNAN S.J., *God and Reason,* Fordham, New York, 1946, P.89

No painter would agree to an art critic's review of his work when a judgment is made by viewing the painting through a magnifying glass, concluding that the painting is ugly. Works of art must be viewed as a whole, according to the intention of the artist; this is called seeing things in their proper perspective.

The great sculptor and painter Michaelangelo, when carving his masterpiece, *the pieta*, purposefully sculpted Jesus out of proportion. A careful eye will catch the slight disproportion between the upper and lower body of Jesus. What Michaelangelo did was make the legs of Jesus proper to a six-foot man, but his upper body proper to a five-foot man. Mary is also much larger than Jesus, almost dwarfing Him. This was necessary in order to depict the image he had in mind. If he had made Jesus and Mary in proper proportion, it would have distorted the sculpture. Michaelangelo was sculpting to convey the sacrificial love and sorrow of the Mother of God, as she held in her arms her Divine Son. He beautifully depicted this in his work, even though in part, in its depiction of the human body, it could be taken as ugly.

The world is God's masterpiece. He is the Supreme Artificer, and we cannot critique from our microcosmic viewpoint what seem to us apparent flaws in the canvas, such as physical evils. If permitting flaws in a part, in order to bring out the perfection and beauty of the whole, can be seen as a trait of genius such as is the case with Michaelangelo, how much more should one consider this with regard to the work of the Creator of the universe? And if we call it beautiful when no man has yet seen it in its entirety, we obviously are in no position to judge the genius of the artist, but only to appreciate and stand in awe.

"Thus I saw and clearly realized that You have made all things good, and that there are no substances not made by You. And because all the things You have made are not equal, they have a goodness (over and above) as a totality: because they are good individually, and they are very good altogether, for our God has made all things very good."[47]

This is the goal of any philosophy-to see reality as far as we can in its full and proper perspective.

The objection is made that God must still have willed evil. To this we point out, that though God certainly permitted physical evil, He did not will it for its own sake *per se,* but *per accidens*[48], that is indirectly, for the sake of the good, the good of the whole universe. This, we have already said implicitly, does not contradict His Goodness, nor should it be held as a weakness on His part.

One could conceive of a world, consisting of artificial trees and plants, which never grow and die, and a multitude of animals that do not eat one another or suffer in any way; a world in which no one would hurt himself but would this

---

[47] ST. AUGUSTINE, *Confessions,* Sheed & Ward, New York, 1942, Bk.7, N.12

[48] See Glossary

be a more perfect world?

It must be mentioned that from the beginning God did will a world that would be without human suffering but because of man's disobedience by original sin creation was thrown into disharmony, hence the present order of things we must deal with as they are today.

> "God forbid that I should say: 'I wished that these things were not'; because even if I saw only them, though I should want better things, yet even for them alone I should praise You. I no longer desired better, because I had thought upon them all and with clearer judgment I realized that while certain higher things are better than lower things, yet all things together are better than the higher alone."[49]

---

[49] St. AUGUSTINE, *Confessions,* Sheed & Ward, New York, 1942, Bk.7, N.13

Moral Evil

The second type of evil *(Moral evil)* pertains to the rational creatures God has made. These rational creatures (angels and man) were endowed with a unique faculty of choice, called the will. With this capacity of freely choosing comes the capacity of going against God, and the nature which He has given us. This is called sinning. Physical evil, we have stated, God wills *indirectly*, by creating a universe, the physical perfection of which requires that some beings be capable of suffering and dying. The same physical perfection of the universe would also require man to be free, but this in no way necessitated man to abuse this freedom by acting contrary to his nature. Hence, God cannot have willed moral evil *in itself*, *(per se)*, or *indirectly*, *(per accidens)*. But since God, in His goodness, does not destroy or reclaim a gift freely given to man, He permits this evil in order to show His power by bringing about a greater good.

God, knowing the future of His rational

creatures actions, foresaw that it was better to allow man the ability to be more like Him than he would be, were he not free. Freely choosing to love and serve God is a source of greater happiness for man. Happiness he could not possess, if he were compelled to love and serve God like a rock held to the ground by the force of gravity.

If someone were planning to have a party, he naturally would invite his friends. He doesn't force them to come, but allows them the choice of coming or declining the invitation, hoping that in their friendship they will join the party. It would be ridiculous to have a party where all were forced to it against their will, or, in foreseeing that some would reject the invitation, to force everyone to go in order to prevent the other few from staying away. No one in their right mind would want forced friendship, but rather friendship based on love, choice, and sacrifice.

The tyranny in the above example is on a small scale found in many forms of social systems, such as communism. They have an ideal of happiness, (usually this means the ideal of the dictator in power), and this theoretical, natural state of happiness is held out in one hand to the ignorant masses, with a whip in the other. It's been tried in the past, yet the lesson seems never to be learned that although everyone desires ultimate happiness, it cannot be shoved down their throats as if there is no free will.

One must realize that no matter how the picture is painted, not everyone will agree as to it's beauty, because the subjective aspect in the appreciation of beauty would demand as many different pictures as people. Of course, we can come close in our agreement about the beautiful as we can about our ultimate happiness, because this agreement is founded on the objective aspect of beauty or happiness, and in our common human nature. This communism can do, by setting forth an ideal which appeals to human nature. The danger lies in exaggerating the appeal of that ideal to man's nature, while excluding what appeals to the individual.

This is what an atheistic system like communism does. It forgets that man is not an existing collective human nature, but that men are existing human persons, sharing a common human nature. In reaching for an ideal called the common good, communism tramples on the person.

Everyone may agree that in order to make an omelet you must first break a few eggs, but not everyone will want the omelet.[50] The only satisfactory state of happiness is one that would fulfill both the objective and subjective criteria needed. This can only be found in a being who is the fullness of perfection, and can communicate this fullness to man.

The bedrock of this reasoning is that God, as God, wants man to share in His life and happiness, and in order to attain to this state of happiness, man has to choose it freely. This freedom means the risk of moral evil, which is in

---

[50] See Page 12, Reference to Communism.

no way willed or caused by God. St. Augustine said it best, that God would in no way permit moral evil in the world, unless by His Omnipotence, He could bring about a greater good in the end[51].

"As a sick man is sometimes made to take bitter medicine or undergo a painful operation to save his life, and these hardships are no evidence of unwisdom in the physician or surgeon, but proofs of the doctor's skill, so the physical ills which may make man, sick and wounded by original sin, sound and strong in spiritual health, are no evidence of unwisdom in the Divine Physician, but evidence of His wondrous skill. As a wise and devoted father may allow his beloved son to feel the consequences of an act of folly, in order that wisdom may come through bitter experience, so the most wise and loving Father of men may allow His

---

[51] ST. AUGUSTINE, *Enchridion*, Gateway Editions, Washington D.C., 1992, Ch11, p.11

children to suffer physical evil (although He is not the cause or author of such evil), in order that they may learn to withdraw their hopes and their trust from things of time and to fix them upon eternal values. We are forced by reason to the conclusion that the existence of physical evils is no argument against Divine Perfection, but, on the contrary, is a proof of such perfection."[52]

It has been shown how evil in the world does not disprove an all-good God, nor is it an adequate reason to jump ship. It may mean he who wishes a solution to the problem and mystery of evil will have to actually face the reality of a little mind work, and even then, not expect to discover all difficulties resolved, especially when we stop at a strictly philosophical analysis. With this, no one is ever completely satisfied, as there is always something of a gap to be filled.

---

[52] Rev. Msgr. Paul J. Glenn S.T.D., *Apologetics,* Tan, Illinois, 1980, P. 103

VI

THE CHRISTIAN CONTRA ATHEISTIC SOLUTION

God always has the last word, even if so many today foolishly believe the contrary. Around 1930 a popular British writer, *Middleton Murray* gave a book length exposition of this error with the title *"Adieu to God"*. G.K. Chesterton wrote the following verses succinctly exposing the simplistic presupposition of so many in dismissing God:

"Murray on finding *le bon Dieu*,
Chose *difficile a croire*,
Illogically said *"Adieu"*,
But God said, *"Au revoir"*.[53]

---

[53] G.K. CHESTERTON, Verses In Collected Works, Vol. X, San Francisco, Part 1, p.508, *Murray on finding the 'good God', a thing hard to believe, Illogically said "By for Good", But God said, "See you again".*

So in line with tradition, we move on to the "Christian contra atheistic solution." As has been stated, many have applied their own pseudo-philosophies to the problem, and have come up short, no matter how clever the proponent of the philosophy. Therefore, no apologies are necessary to open the mind to the fresh air of Christian wisdom, taught by the doctors and fathers of the Church, developing clearly the major principles of the Church's unchanging doctrine. Like the tools of a fine lapidarian they are disposed instruments of God artfully engraving these principles into the minds of those desiring and searching for the truth.

Moral evil is a harsh reality, affecting even the amount of physical evil seen in the world. And with global communication, the knowledge of pain and suffering is thrown into the laps of children, saturating them with issues hard enough for adults to handle. There were times before mass media when the amount of evil seen was tempered considerably because of the relative isolation of villages. When a neighbor's house burned down, all would pitch in and help out in whatever way they could. The suffering was just as real, but there was always a feeling of solidarity, and a tangible means of showing compassion, built on a hope in God, who guides everything in His goodness.

Presently, a high school student can go home, watch three or four wars enfolding before his eyes, see plane crashes killing hundreds, natural disasters such as hurricanes, forest fires, and earthquakes, and famines, children killing each other, mothers killing their children, and to top it all off, the O-zone layer crises, rain forest depletion, and the ever growing endangered species list. All this takes place before the evening meal with the family. There's no sense of solidarity, and no tangible means of showing compassion for suffering all over the globe, which leads people to become desensitized, not just to global suffering, but to the suffering closest to home as well, as this suffering often pales in comparison.

Since we live in a world with its back turned

away from God, even a word about God and a prayer in school is silenced. And when most children haven't seen the inside of a church or a catechism book, obviously there is not much *hope* being fostered. Rather a subtle feeling of despair pervades everything; hence the rate of suicide plaguing society. If they do not give in to despair, many turn stoic toward life, an attitude taking as its premise, "If you care, you only get hurt, because life is cruel; the only way to confront it is resignation in a comfortably numb apathy".

It's not a revelation to understand why evil is such a harsh reality to comprehend both intellectually and emotionally. The hard fact is, we are bankrupt without God, and the problem of evil can never be resolved solely on a natural basis. History can confirm that fact. Many would argue that our God is bankrupt Himself, because it seems that those who have faith in Him suffer the most while they persevere in (vain) hope that God will come through to save them. There was a prisoner in Auschwitz who constantly exhorted his fellow prisoners to keep faith in God who would not fail them. He held to his convictions, until it was his turn to be packed inside the gas chamber. It was then that he cried out, "There is no God!"[54] It seems from a worldly point of view that he finally saw the cold yet logical reality. The fundamental problem with the prisoner was the same as that of Job's friends who ridiculed him in his suffering; that the amount of material prosperity enjoyed on earth is the criteria for judging one's friendship with God (consequently God is only as good as the thickness of one's wallet). If you are well off in this life, then God is rewarding you for your faithfulness, but if you are destitute, God is punishing you for your infidelity. This erroneous thinking led the prisoner to despair when he felt his faithfulness wasn't rewarded, because if he were to judge himself according to his own theology, he would have to conclude he was a sinner and was being punished by God. This he couldn't do, so rather than deny his own integrity, he would deny God's. Some would suggest that this would be the

---

[54] PETER KREEFT, *Making sense out of Suffering,* Servant Books, Ann Arbor Michigan, 1986, p.30

conclusion of all those who believe in God when faced with a death camp, where all their intellectual arguments and faith would fall to pieces.

This is not true of a Catholic priest named Maximilian Kolbe, who gave up his life for a fellow prisoner who, with nine other men, was condemned to die in a starvation bunker in Auschwitz. His life and death contradicted all natural explanation and brought about a good in the face of evil, while granting him no reward or consolation, from a materialist point of view. What is in the Christian faith, that one can face death head on, not viewing death as an end, but merely as an obstacle, similar to the mountain a climber faces.

The Cross

The Catholic solution to suffering in the world is, to put it plainly, 'the Cross'. We must recall the reason why the Cross stands as the solution. Adam, representing all mankind, freely chose to disobey God, abusing the gift of free will.

God's Justice required that restitution be made for this evil, so He exiled man from his earthly paradise. Though not annihilating him on the spot, which would have not only solved the problem of moral evil, but also eliminated all complaints of evil in the world, He did require that death and physical suffering would be the consequence of the sin. But, by an act of His mercy, He promised to redeem man and clean up the mess man made of His harmonious creation, and to repair the relation of man to Himself, also disrupted by sin.

The point here is that, since the fall of our first parents, history and revelation have shown that God has done nothing but lift man out of the dirt into which he continually falls. The commonly asked question, "Why do bad things always happen to good people?" assumes that there are good people, when the truth is that none of us are good, in the strict sense of the word. Most suffering directly results from human sin, even when divine punishment is involved. We cannot fathom the gratuity of God, Who, being rejected by His creatures, redeems them by becoming man,

"Humbling Himself by sharing in our humanity in order that we may share in His divinity[55]".

Not satisfied with the infinite humility of becoming man, He also suffered death by crucifixion, whereby the ultimate evil of Deicide became the ultimate source of good for man. It was precisely by this death that the gates of paradise were laid open, and the reality of suffering was seen in a new light. Only in this light of the cross, does suffering have any meaning at all. The suffering of the Son of God becomes God's solution to our difficulties and complaints. What we see in this new light is the temporal character of suffering. It does not last forever, and is offered to us as a result of Christ's sacrifice.

Not every aspect and avenue of the mystery of the Cross and its meaning for human suffering can be explored and scrutinized in a booklet as

---

[55] Roman Rite, *Novus Ordo*, Sacramentary, Liturgy of the Eucharist, "Through the mystery of this water and wine may we come to share in the Divinity of Christ who humbled himself by sharing in our humanity."

brief as this.   But the main point that can be emphasized here is, in Christian eyes, the form of evil called suffering does not point the blame at God, but at us. The Cross upon which we hung God Himself, is at once a quickening of the mind *to* the consequences of abusing free-will by sin, and *to the remedy* of that abuse, which is the same Cross.

The mystery of God's goodness to men is the act of redemption, not for any gain of His own, as He is perfect and self-sufficient, needing nothing from His creatures to fulfill Him in any way, but because He wills that man should gain and simply share in His glory.

We must not think of God as we do of men, for frequently the motives underlying man's actions are selfish.   But we should understand God as His Son has revealed Him, as One who clothes the lilies of the field and feeds the birds of the sky with such care, that not one of them falls to the ground without His knowledge.   And are not we also to be cared for, who are much more than these[56]?

Another aspect of human suffering in the light of the cross, teaches us the suffering offered to God and on behalf of God, is meritorious and salvific when united to Christ's suffering. "I make up what is lacking in the sufferings of Christ[57]." Suffering can be purifying, leading us to prayer and closer union with God. Without some evil in the world, much good would be lost, such as heroic virtues when one is faced with trials, cruelty and adversity. We do not know how these sufferings are used by God, and will not, until we are in heaven, but we do know that they are used. God has so ordered everything, that while we are in this vale of tears, suffering can be, in a way, an answer for suffering.

We see this in the lives of the saints who, in voluntarily taking suffering upon themselves elevated the suffering of others, as in the case with St. Maximilian Kolbe, and most efficaciously in

---

[56] St. Matthew 6:28

[57] St. Paul, Colossians 1:24

the suffering of Our Lady who, in her innocence, accepted and offered to God, the suffering caused her by the cruel death of her Son, not for her own sanctification, but for us, as the condition for the salvation and sanctification of others.

The prophet Isaiah summed up all that has been said until now so accurately, it is as if he was there to witness it. Rightly he is called the 5th evangelist.

"See my servant shall prosper, he shall be raised high and greatly exalted. Even as many were amazed at him, so marred was his look beyond that of man, and his appearance beyond that of mortals, so shall he startle many nations, because of him kings shall stand speechless; for those who have not been told shall see, those who have not heard shall ponder it...", "There was in him not stately bearing to make us look at him, not appearance that would attract us to him. He was spurned and avoided by men, a man of suffering, accustomed to infirmity, one of those from whom men hide their faces spurned, and we held him in no esteem. Yet it was our infirmities that he bore, our suffering that he endured, while we thought of him as stricken, as one smitten by God and afflicted. But he was pierced for our offenses, crushed for our sins; upon him was the chastisement that makes us whole, by his stripes we were healed. We had all gone astray like sheep, each following his own way; but the Lord laid upon him the guilt of us all. Though he was harshly treated, he submitted and opened not his mouth; like a lamb led to the slaughter or a sheep before the shearers; he was silent and opened not his mouth. Oppressed and condemned, he was taken away, and who would have thought any more of his destiny? When he was cut off from the land of the living, and smitten for the sin of his people, a grave was assigned him among the wicked and a burial place with evildoers, though he had done no wrong nor spoken any falsehood. (But the Lord was pleased to crush him in infirmity.) If he gives his life as an offering for sin, he shall see his descendents in a long life, and the will of the Lord shall be accomplished through him.   Because of his affliction he shall see the light in fullness of days; through his suffering, my servant shall justify many, and their guilt he shall bear. Therefore I will give him his portion among the great, and he shall divide the spoils with the mighty, because he surrendered himself to death and was counted among the wicked; and he shall take away the sins of many, and win pardon for their offenses." (Isaiah52: 13-15), (53:1-12)

VII
CONCLUSION:
GOD OR NOTHING!

Only in God is found a Solution to the Mystery of Evil

After some reflection on the nature of evil, that it is a privation, not some exaggerated principle existing in itself, equal and opposed to the good, it is relatively easy to put evil into perspective intellectually, but as a general rule does not make it any easier to tolerate. That is why, on a natural basis, evil can never be fully understood or explained, especially when that form of evil is human suffering, for that is the core of the matter. It is hard to see loved ones suffer through no fault of their own, and then to see those who lead wicked lives prosper and not ask "why?" This is common ground, shared by believer and non-believer alike, but where they depart makes all the difference in the world. St. Maximilian M. Kolbe, OFM Conv., gave an interesting explanation to this problem that was posed to him:

> **Problem:** I have often heard it said that God is very unjust to let wicked people prosper, while many good people do not have it so good.

> *Answer:* If the person who raises this objection were to first demonstrate that there is no after-life (which he can never do), then perhaps he might have some kind of a case. Those who are convinced of God's Providence regarding the after-life easily answer this problem. The good and correct answer is that the wicked do not prosper more than the good in the long run, because God sends those unrepentant of their wickedness to hell.

> "**N:** Ordinarily good people suffer,

whereas most of the time wicked people seem to get by rather well. Where is God's justice?

K: God is infinitely just. Otherwise He would not be God. Consequently He must reward every good action and punish every bad one. No deed, no word, no thought escapes His judgment. Now, is there in the world any person who is completely bad in everything, who never does anything good in his life?

N: Nobody is like that.

K: At least some time or other everyone fulfills a duty well, either showing kindness to his neighbor, or managing to do some other good deed. Now, if such a man, seriously transgressing other commandments, deserved to go to hell after his death, when would it have been possible for God to reward the little good he did?..

N: In this life.

K: Now let me ask again: Is there any person perhaps, even among the best, who has always done everything well? *(Except Our Lord and His Immaculate Mother.)*

N: No, there is no one like that.

K: Agreed. For we have the maxim: *The just man falls seven times a day. (Prov. 24:16).* Now if God wants to shorten his purgatory or grant him paradise as soon as he dies, how will justice be satisfied for the person's misdeeds?

N: I see! You are showing me how things must be.

K: God shows a special love for those whom he punishes in this world. Purgatory is a long heavy punishment. But if we willingly accept the crosses of this life, we will earn all the more glory in paradise with less purgatory. Hence the proverb, *Whom God loves, he chastises (Prov. 3:12)*. Therefore wicked people are not to be envied who enjoy an easy life. Rather, we and they ought to take great alarm at the thought that this fact may mean that they have already had their reward for the little good they have done."(From Scritti Kolbe, 1050)[58]

To take up the view of the Atheist by denying God, is to choose to perceive a reality that goes against mankind's very nature, flattening everything out to a temporal and futile existence, in which everything happens by chance. When man begins to interpret man according to animal existence, ignoring his transcendence of mere animality by his rational nature, suffering becomes absolutely intolerable. It is something to be avoided and not endured, because there is no hope

---

[58] FR. BASIL M. ARTHADEVA, FI, STL, *Current errors and their refutation*, problem #1 p.387, *In Christ to the World*.Vol.35,(1990)

in a higher good or afterlife. Man looks to himself as the answer to the problem of evil, which he equates solely with human suffering.

The results, as we have already explained previously in this booklet, are the grasping at earthly utopias, and in running from suffering he leaves a wake of it behind him, never reaching his longed for natural state of happiness.

Those who do not go so far as to deny the existence of God, but who do not accept Him in all His attributes (pantheists, manicheans and deists) have something in common with atheists; intellectual dishonesty.

The views or theories above all take a position that amounts to high sounding excuses, using a facade of rhetoric to clothe their intellectual arguments with persuasiveness, and to justify their immorality. To invert a phrase of Ludwig Feuerbach, (1804-1872)[59], if there were no such

---

[59] Scott Hahn; Tape series, *Where's God in an ungodly world*, St. Josephs Communications, tape#1; L. Feuerbach coined a popular line among Atheists,

thing as Atheism, we'd invent it anyway, and that's what we did.

Keeping divine law reflected in the natural law given to every man in the form of conscience, by which we discern what *ought* to be done from what *ought* not to be done, is difficult, and those who tend to break the law also tend to justify themselves by rationalizing their actions in order to be rid of that thorn in the side called guilt, pricking them to heed the voice of conscience. "The fool says in his heart there is no God",[60] and the foundation is laid for practical Atheism or in other words, living a lie. I call this to live a lie, because in order to maintain it, one must take a view that goes contrary to the heart of truth, against the ostensive evidence of a reality permeated with God, who is at once Creator and Governor of this well ordered universe, to which chance plays no part. That is to echo St. Paul in his letter to the Romans[61], to be quoted at length,

---

"If there was no God, we'd invent Him anyway," supposedly out of man's need.

[60] Psalm14:1

[61] Romans 1:18-32

because of the forcible common sense with which he treats the problem of evil, from its source; the consequences of a philosophy which ostracizes God from the minds of men.

"The wrath of God is revealed from heaven against all ungodliness and wickedness of those men who in wickedness **hold back the truth** of God seeing that what may be known about God is manifest to them. For God has manifested it to them"[62]

This reflects the theme of the book of Wisdom,[63] which bluntly states that godless people like Pharaoh in Egypt become similar to a senseless infant, taking as gods the most worthless and disgusting beasts, even after God manifested Himself to them. So the wrath of God was revealed by leaving them to be tortured by the very things they deemed to be gods, so that they might recognize the true God. But, persevering

---

[62] *ibid.*, 1:18-20
[63] Wisdom 3:23-27; Chap.13

in their obstinacy and refusal to know God their final condemnation came. St. Paul continues saying,

> "… That they are without excuses, because while the invisible attributes of God were clearly visible and understood through the things He has made, so that although they knew God, they did not glorify Him as God or give thanks, but became vain in their reasoning, and their senseless minds have been darkened for while professing to be wise they have become fools."[64]

Recalling the plight of those who turn away from God, he writes,

> "They exchanged the truth of God for a lie, and worshipped and served the creature rather than the Creator who is blessed forever, amen."[65]

---

[64] Romans 1:23-30
[65] *ibid.*, 1:30-32

Atheists may profess unbelief in God, but as St. Paul explains they do have their gods in denying the true God. In effect, they set themselves or nature up as god. It is in this that they live a lie, putting on blinders to a spiritual order, and in this, they are to blame, not for their ignorance, which is somewhat pardonable, but for their intention of holding back the truth.

The solution of St. Paul to the atheist's position is not some technical philosophical argument of which he was surely capable of producing, but is to point out that on a consistent basis, those who deny God refute themselves by the utter chaos which their system is reduced to. Man, in crying out that he is oppressed by religion in its tyrannical authority, such as a concept of God subjects him to, supposedly breaks free into higher nobility trying to become his own master. God respecting their decision, deserts them, and in their newfound freedom, they degenerate into brutes, now oppressed by fallen nature and unnatural vice.

This is the conclusion we must reasonably make, because although we see human suffering in the world, we must humbly accept that there are some things that man cannot rationally explain, not because there is no answer to the mystery of evil, but because right here and now, we cannot presume to stand in judgment, interpreting God's reasons for permitting certain evil, unless He reveals it to us. The Christian knows He has revealed it to us, through His only begotten Son, who died on the cross, conquering and shedding light, even on that mysterious thing called death, which all natural human speculations cannot penetrate.

We recall the words God spoke to Job:

"Will we have arguing with the Almighty by the critic? Let him who would correct God give answer!"[66]

Job's reply to the Lord:

"I know that you can do all things, and that

---

[66] Job 40:2

no purpose of yours can be hindered. I have dealt with great things that I do not understand things to wonderful for me, which I cannot know. I had heard of you by word of mouth but now my eye has seen you and I disown what I have said and repent in dust and ashes."[67]

---

[67] *ibid.*, 42:2-6

VII
POST SCRIPT

*The Spiritual Motherhood of Mary as
the Solution to the Mystery of Suffering
and the Providence of God.*

A careful, but by no means excessively difficult reflection, shows us how reasonable the catholic belief in Divine Providence really is, that belief centers in the mystery of the Cross. It gives the only reasonable analysis of suffering and sin (moral and physical evil) an analysis that begins with the disobedience of our first parents opening the door to the punishment of suffering and death, then concludes with the crucifixion, death and resurrection of Jesus Christ.

Our Lord overcame suffering and death at

its root- sin, enabling us to live and grow in the state of sanctifying grace then ultimately enter into the beatific vision for all eternity, victorious over death in our resurrected bodies.

Although Jesus overcame suffering and death it does not mean that he abolished the inevitability of physical suffering which in one form or another is part of man's very existence. Our Lord changes the very meaning of suffering or one could say He gives meaning to the suffering we endure so that it can be salvific and noble. As such despair is replaced with hope which in turn produces a joy and peace despite the sufferings we undergo.

Our Holy Father Pope John Paul II addresses this point in his general audience on Wednesday, Feb. 11th, 2004.

"From a merely human standpoint, pain and sickness can appear absurd realities: but when we let the light of the Gospel shine on them we succeed in understanding their deep salvific meaning. 'From the paradox of the Cross', I stressed in my Message for today's world day of the sick, springs the answer to our most worrying questions- <u>Christ suffers for us.</u> He takes upon himself the sufferings of everyone and redeems them- <u>Christ suffers with us,</u> enabling us to share our pain with him. United to the suffering of Christ, human suffering becomes a means of salvation".

Our Holy Father's reflection on the salvific meaning of suffering is an echo of what the first Pope St. Peter taught before him.

"Christ suffered for you and left you an example to have you follow in his footsteps. He did no wrong; no deceit was found in his mouth when he was insulted, he returned no insult. When he was made to suffer, he did not counter with threats. Instead he delivered himself up to the one who judges justly. In his own body he brought your sins to the Cross, so that all of us, dead to sin, could live in accord with God's Will. By his wounds you were healed."[68]

St. Peter says that Christ left us an example of patience in suffering and Our Lord makes it clear that as Christians we will suffer, as he himself did.

"They will lay hands on you and persecute you, delivering you up to the synagogues and prisons, and you will be brought before kings and governors for my name's sake. This will be a time for you to bear testimony. Settle it therefore in your minds, not to meditate beforehand how to answer: for I will give you a mouth and wisdom, which none of your adversaries will be able to withstand or contradict. You will be delivered up even by parents and brothers and kinsmen and friends, and some of you they will put to death; you will be hated by all for

---

[68] 1 Pet 2:21b-24

my name's sake. But not a hair of your head will perish. By your endurance you will gain your lives".[69]

Jesus did not water down the imperative binding his true followers to accept with an act of faith and the exercise of patience, hardships and trials because he changed the reality of suffering into something good that good being its salvific character. Pope John Paul II in his Apostolic letter on the Christian meaning of human suffering, Salvifici Doloris, reveals how we being followers of Christ should view suffering by making use of the phrase 'the Gospel of suffering' or in other words the good news of suffering. From the Cross, this good news of the salvific character of suffering is offered to us as something to be embraced in imitation of Christ.

The gospel of suffering-the Cross, is what became an obstacle to the Gentiles and a stumbling block to the Jews, spurned by them as foolishness and an absurdity, it is not to be spurned

---

[69] Lk 21:12-19

by followers of Christ.[70] To spurn suffering in its salvific character is to reject the Cross and to reject the Cross is to reject the foundation of Christianity not to mention to be ashamed of its founder Our Lord Jesus Christ himself.

This flight from the Cross is characteristic of our modern age and of many Christians who whether in word or deed pretend that Christianity can somehow be divorced from the Cross.

There remains one final question: how does one come to embrace the Cross in practice as distinct from acknowledging the reasonableness of the theory?

"The world is a mystery, life, time, death, doubt, good and evil, and the uncertainty which hangs about our eternal lot, are all mysteries. They lie burning on the heart at times. But the Crucifix is the meaning of them, the solution of them

---

[70] cf. 1 Cor 1:23-24

all. It puts the question and answers it as well…No wonder saints have hung over their Crucifixes in such trances of contented love. **But Mary is a part of the reality of this symbol.** The mother and the Apostle stand, as it were, through all ages at the foot of the Crucifix, symbols themselves of the great mystery of the sole true religion of what God has done for the world which he created. As we cannot think of the child at Bethlehem without his mother, so neither will the Gospel let us picture to ourselves the man on Calvary without his mother also."[71]

Look once again at the scene on Golgatha on that Friday of Holy Week- and by extension on the "Good Friday" of every life and you will see not only the crucified savior, but the woman who is his mother and whom he gave to us as our mother. That gift has one primary purpose: to enable us by baptism to become her children, his

---

[71] Fr. Frederick William Faber, D.D., *The Foot of The Cross,* Tan, Illinois, 1978, Pg. 240

brethren, to sustain us therefore in sharing his passion and death as she once sustained him in his sacrifice of his life and so come to the glory of the Resurrection as we behold it already in her assumption and coronation. Fr. Frederick William Faber writes that there can hardly be a shade of sorrow which is not familiar to Mary's heart and that she is by her experience the great doctoress in the science of sorrow:

> "Indeed, her sorrows upon Calvary were the very birth-throes in which all men were born as Mary's Children, and thus her compassion was not merely a fitness to be our mother, but her very delivery of us as her children. As it was in her compassion that we were born to her, as it is in her compassion that we find our motives for filial confidence in her during life, so it was in her compassion that we gained our right to die in her maternal arms. For it was then that she herself received the right of the patronage of deathbeds, because of her attendance at the deathbed of Our lord; and her

ministry to us, as to Him, in the hour of death is part of her office upon which the Church dwells most strongly by naming it in the Ave Maria. Thus is her compassion inseparably bound up in the manifold offices of mercy which, by the ordinance of God, Mary discharges to us".[72]

Our Lord desired to identify Mary with himself in everything; His life, His mission of salvation of souls, His passion, death and resurrection. This is in no way an exaggeration, it is reality, the Natural Son of God became truly the Son of Mary and She became and is the Mother of God. Once we assert this truth is it not an understatement to say that Our Lord wished to identify Our Lady with himself in his life and mission and through her, all men?

"This is not all: the divine Redeemer wishes to penetrate the soul of every

---

[72] Fr. Frederick William Faber, *At the Foot of the Cross,* Tan, Illinois, 1978

sufferer through the heart of His holy Mother, the first and the most exalted of all the redeemed. As though by a continuation of that motherhood which by the power of the Holy Spirit had given Him life, the dying Christ conferred upon the ever Virgin Mary a new kind of motherhood-spiritual and universal-towards all human beings, so that every individual, during the pilgrimage of faith, might remain, together with her, closely united to him unto the Cross, and so that every form of suffering, given fresh life by the power of this Cross, should become no longer the weakness of man but the power of God."[73]

By being born a man Our Lord identified Himself with all men so that by his death and resurrection we might through baptism, that rebirth of water and the Spirit, become adopted sons of God, his brethren and children of Mary.

---

[73] POPE JOHN PAUL II, Apostolic Letter, *Salvifici Doloris,* Pauline, Boston, 1984, n. 26

Death entered the world through the sin of Eve making her the mother of all the dead because spiritually we were dead and physically bound to die. Life entered the world through Mary because she is the mother of the giver and author of life. Through baptism we enter into and partake of this life, consequently, Mary becomes our mother in the spiritual order. As in the biological order motherhood does not cease at birth but continues for the whole life of the child so in the order of grace spiritual motherhood does not end with baptism but continues even into eternity. The ways by which Mary exercises her role as mother are many, but they are especially evident in her solicitude for those who suffer.

It is no coincidence that twenty years ago on the memorial of Our Lady of Lourdes Our Holy Father John Paul II published his Apostolic Letter, Salvifici Doloris, On the Christian Meaning of Human Suffering. He informs us of the reason after the concelebrated Mass in St. Peter's addressing the sick persons present on the occasion of the memorial of Our lady of Lourdes and the 12th world day of the sick, February 11th, 2004.

"In looking at Mary our hearts are opened to hope, for in her we see the great things God accomplishes when we render ourselves humbly available to doing his will. The Immaculate Virgin is a marvelous sign of the victory of life over death, of love over sin, of salvation over every physical and spiritual ailment. She is a sign of comfort and never failing hope (cf. Lumen Gentium n. 68). What we admire already fulfilled in her is a pledge of what God wants to give to every human creature: fullness of life, joy and peace".[74]

In another address he gave this message for The 12th World Day of the Sick, December 1st, 2003.

"If Jesus is the source of life which defeats death, Mary is the caring mother who meets the hopes of her children by obtaining for them the health of their

---

[74] POPE JOHN PAUL II, *Jesus, Mary, Hope,* L'Osservatore Romano, February 18th, 2004

souls and bodies."[75]

Then again on the 11th of February 2004 in a Wednesday audience the Holy Father gave this message,

"'*Sub tuum praesidium*', as we prayed at the beginning of our meeting, 'Under your protection we seek refuge', Immaculate Virgin of Lourdes, who present yourself to us as the perfect model of creation according to God's original plan. To you we entrust the sick, the elderly, the lonely; soothe their pain, dry their tears and obtain for each one the strength they need to do God's will.

May you support those who toil every day to alleviate the sufferings of their brethren! And help us all to grow in the knowledge of Christ, who by his death

---

[75] POPE JOHN PAUL II, *Health is harmony of body and soul in Christ,* L'Osservatore Romano, February 18th, 2004, Pg. 7

and Resurrection defeated the powers of evil and death".[76]

Through Christ's Resurrection and Mary's Assumption and Coronation we have been given a pledge of future glory and a happiness that will never end. In the book of revelation we read about those who have persevered and come out of the great tribulation-that 'Good Friday' and Calvary in everyone's life:

"They shall hunger no more neither thirst anymore; the sun shall not strike them, nor any scorching heat. For the Lamb in the midst of the throne will be their shepherd and he will guide them to springs of living water; and God will wipe every tear from their eyes".[77]

By giving to us a Mother, God is anticipating the consolation of eternity, for even now she

---

[76] POPE JOHN PAUL II, *Our Lady of Lourdes, pray for us!*, L'Osservatore Romano, February 18th, 2004, Pg. 11

[77] Rev. 7:16-17

begins to wipe the tears from our eyes. In reverence and awe for this gift of God's providence, we proclaim with the Apostle:

> "Oh, the depth of the riches of the wisdom and of the knowledge of God! How incomprehensible are His judgments and how unsearchable His ways! For "Who has known the mind of the Lord, or who has been His counselor? Or who has first given to Him, that recompense should be made him?" For from Him and through Him and unto Him are all things. To Him be the glory forever!"[78]

To the question how does one live the mystery of Divine Providence, viz., the Cross, the answer is: become like little children, become children of Mary especially by consecration to her in imitation of the beloved disciple St. John who took Mary into his home. Behold your mother (cf. Jn 19:26) is the concrete realization of Mt

---

[78] Rom. 11:33-36

18:2-3;

"And calling to him a child, he put him in the midst of them, and said, 'Truly, I say to you, unless you become like children, you will never enter the kingdom of heaven'".[79]

And also of Mt.11:25;

"At that time Jesus declared, 'I thank thee Father, Lord of heaven and earth that thou hast hidden these things from the wise and understanding and revealed them to babes; yes, Father, for such was thy gracious will.'"[80]

---

[79] Mt 18:2-3
[80] Mt 11:25

GLOSSARY

Albigensianism:[81] A modified form of the Manichaean heresy that flourished in Southern France in the twelfth and thirteenth centuries. It claimed that a good deity created the world of the spirit, and an evil god the material world, including the human body, which is under its control. The good deity sent Jesus Christ, as a creature, to deliver human souls from their imprisonment. Albigensians favored suicide and advocated abstaining from marriage. A crusade was organized against them as a menace to society, and was opposed by Raymond of Toulouse. In Belgium, France, and Germany the war against them continued even after their defeat, contrary to the wishes of Pope Innocent III. By the fifteenth

---

[81] FR. JOHN A. HARDON S.J., *Modern Catholic Dictionary*, Eternal Life, Kentucky, 2001

century they had disappeared as a political force, but their Manichaean ideas reappeared in the in the reformation.

A Priori:[82] From what is before, that is, from cause to effect. Reasoning from principles to conclusions, or from prior knowledge to consequences; therefore deduction. A basic premise of Catholic morality in applying general norms to specific practice.

Atheism:[83] Denial of a personal God who is totally distinct from the world he created. Modern atheism has become so varied and widespread that the Second Vatican Council identified no less than eight forms of disbelief under the single term *atheismus*: "Some people expressly deny the existence of God. Others maintain that man cannot make any assertion whatsoever about Him. Still others admit only such methods of investigation as would make it seem quite

---

[82]*ibid.*
[83]*ibid.*

meaningless to ask questions about God.[84] Many, trespassing beyond the boundaries of the positive sciences, either contend that everything can be explained by the reasoning process used in such sciences, or, on the contrary, hold that there is no such thing as absolute truth. With others it is their exaggerated idea of man that causes their faith to languish; they are more prone, it would seem, to affirm man than to deny God. Yet others have such a faulty notion of God that when they disown this product of the imagination their denial has no reference to the God of the Gospels. There are also those who never inquire about God; religion never seems to trouble or interest them at all, nor do they try to see why they should bother about it" (*Church in the Modern World*, I, 19). In the light of this array of infidelity, it was

---

[84] Those methods of investigation alluded to are the normal methods used in science when applied to finding the natural causes of material things but have no place as means of determining the reality of God's existence. God is pure spirit and should not be brought as low as something material. He cannot be sought and discovered by a microscope nor proved real by a litmus test. Those who admit of such methods of investigation do in fact make meaningless a true search for God.

only logical for the Council to declare that atheism is one of the greatest problems facing mankind in the world today. (Etym. Greek *atheos*, denying the gods, without a god)

Cathari:[85] A name applied to various Manichaean sects of the later Middle Ages. The essential tenet of their belief was philosophical dualism. There were two ultimate principles, really two creator gods, one of good and the other of evil. They denied the value of oaths and the right to punish, commended suicide, and rejected marriage. Their ideas tended to undermine the foundations of civil society, and for this reason they were opposed not only by the Church but also by the State. By the fourteenth century Catharism had practically disappeared in France, Germany, and England and by the next century in Italy and the Balkans, where it had previously flourished.

Christian Science:[86] A popular name for the

---

[85] *ibid.*

[86] REV. PETER J. STRAVINSKAS, *Catholic Dictionary,* Our Sunday Visitor, Indiana, 1993

beliefs of the Church of Christ Scientist, based in Boston, Mass., this is a system of philosophy and therapy developed by Mary Baker Eddy (1821-1910), who maintained that Scripture teaches that such things as disease, pain, and sin are merely illusionary and will disappear when confronted with spiritual truth. According to this teaching, healing is achieved not through medicine but through correct thought. Christian Science is based upon the belief that the material world is unreal and that man's true nature is solely spiritual; this teaching is outlined and developed in Mrs. Eddy's book *Science and Health*, published originally in 1875.

Communism:[87] The social doctrine that affirms the community of goods and denies the right to ownership of private property. As analyzed in numerous papal documents since Pope Pius IX in 1846, Communism is based on a philosophy, a theory of history, and a definable strategy or methodology. The philosophy is dialectical materialism, which claims that matter and not

---

[87] FR. JOHN A. HARDON S.J., *Modern Catholic Dictionary*, Eternal Life, Kentucky, 2001

spirit, and least of all the infinite Spirit who is God, is the primary reality in the universe; and that material forces in conflict (dialectic) explain all the progress in the world. The Communist theory of history claims that economics is the sole basis of human civilization, making all ethical, religious, philosophical, artistic, social, and political ideas the result of economic conditions. The strategy of Communism is a shifting expediency that defies analysis but has two constants that never really change: massive indoctrination of the people and ruthless suppression of any ideas or institutions that threaten totalitarian control by the Communist Party.

Deism.[88] The theory that accepts the existence of God on purely rational grounds but denies, doubts or rejects as incredible Christianity as a supernatural religion. Accordingly revelation, miracles, grace, and mysteries are excluded from acceptance by what is called "the rational man." Yet deism differs from rationalism in stressing its

---

[88] *ibid.*

acceptance of a personal God and Adherence to what is called natural religion, but with no recognition of a supernatural order. (Etym. Latin *Deus*, God.)

Exemplar[89]*:* Model, idea; that form which the agent deliberately imitates in his action; the original form or idea in whose likeness something can be made; that which causes by guiding action according to a preconceived plan.

Feminism:[90] A system of thought that seeks the same social, political, and economic rights for women as those exercised by men. Authentic Christian feminism advocates these rights within the scriptural and traditional, "in the main", understanding of the differences between men and women as created by God, whereas most radical feminism seeks to obliterate these differences by viewing them as being artificially imposed by a "patriarchal" understanding of society.

---

[89] BERNARD WUELLNER, S.J., *Dictionary of Scholastic Philosophy,* Bruce, 1956

[90] *ibid.*

Idealism:[91] In the philosophy of Plato it is the theory that the visible things of this world are merely copies of the perfect realities of another, supersensible world of the spirit. In St. Augustine and the Scholastics it is the doctrine that the ideal or exemplar according to which everything is made is the idea in the mind of God. In modern philosophy idealism is the theory that denies reality to the external, physical world and attributes real existence only to things as they are in the mind. In its extreme form it is pure subjectivism, denying existence to anything outside the mind of the thinking person.

Jansenism:[92] A system of grace developed by Cornelis Jansen (1585-1638), theologian at Louvain and later Bishop of Ypres. As a school of theology, it should be seen in two stages, namely, the original position of Jansenius and its later development by his followers. Jansenius' own teaching is contained in the book *Augustinus*, which he spent years in writing and was published

---

[91] *ibid.*

[92] *ibid.*

two years after his death. According to Jansenius, man's free will is incapable of any moral goodness. All man's actions proceed either from earthly desires, which stem from concupiscence, or from heavenly desires, which are produced by grace. Each exercises an urgent influence on the human will, which in consequence of its lack of freedom always follows the pressure of the stronger desire. Implicit in Jansenism is the denial of the supernatural order, because on a practical level as all of us know the sensual appetites or concupiscence exerts the stronger desire and many are they who go that way. The reasoning is very simple; we live immoral lives because there is no grace to overpower the sensual passions and if there were grace predominately at work we would not have the possibility of either rejection or acceptance of that grace. Accordingly those who receive the grace will be saved; they are the predestined. All others will be Lost. Jansenism was condemned as heretical in five major propositions by Pope Innocent X in 1653. It was recondemned by Pope Alexander VII in 1656, when Jansenists claimed that their doctrine was misrepresented.

Manichaeism:[93] A dualistic heresy initiated in the third century by a Persian named Mani, Manes, or Manicaeus (215-75) He was considered divinely inspired, and he gained a large following. In the Manichaean system there are two ultimate sources of creation, the one good and the other evil. God is the creator of all that is good, and Satan of all that is evil. Man's spirit is from God; his body is from the devil. There is a constant struggle between the forces of good and those of evil. Good triumphs over evil only insofar as spirit rises superior to the body. In practice Manichaeism denies human responsibility for the evil that one does, on the premise that this is not due to one's own free will but to the dominance of Satan's power in one's life.

Metaphysics:[94] The science of being, as being; or of the absolutely first principles of being. Also called ontology, first philosophy, the philosophy of being, the philosophy of first causes, wisdom. (Etym. Greek *meta*, after, beyond + *physika*, physics.)

---

[93] *ibid.*

[94] *ibid.*

Pantheism:[95] Any of a variety of views that claim that all things are divine, or that God and the universe are really identical, or that there is ultimately no real distinction between God and what believers in creation call the world. It is opposed to the Catholic doctrine that God is present in all things as the cause of their being, without being identical with their substance. (Etym. Greek *Pan*, all + *Theos*, god.)

Per accidens:[96] Latin phrase. 1. *Literally.* "by an accident," "by means of an accident." 2. Accidental or accidentally, q.v. 3. Contingently, q.v. 4. Indirect or indirectly, q.v. Opposite-*per se*. Uses- *per accidens* cause, conversion, effect, intelligible, sensible, etc.

Per se:[97] Literally "by itself" or "through itself." A very common expression in scholastic philosophy and theology to describe something

---

[95] *ibid.*

[96] BERNARD WUELLNER, S.J., *Dictionary of Scholastic Philosophy,* Bruce, Milwaukee, 1956

[97] FR. JOHN A. HARDON S.J., *Modern Catholic Dictionary,* Eternal Life, Kentucky, 2001

by reason of what it is in itself or its own nature without reference to its relationship to other things or the circumstances associated with an object or activity. Thus every human act, "*per se*," is a moral act because it proceeds from the fee will, but it may be either morally good or morally bad. The opposite is "*per accidens.*"

Philosophy:[98] Literally the love of wisdom. It is the science in which natural reason, apart from divine revelation, seeks to understand all things by knowledge of their first causes. (Etym. Greek *philein*, to love + *sophia*, wisdom: *philosophus*.)

Scholastic Philosophy (scholasticism):[99] The system of philosophy and theology first developed in the medieval schools of Christian Europe, having a scholastic or technical language and methodology, building on the writings of the Church Fathers, notably St. Augustine (354-430), using many of the philosophical principles and insights of Aristotle and Neoplatonism, and co-

---

[98] *ibid.*
[99] *ibid.*

ordinated into a synthesis of human and divine wisdom by St. Thomas Aquinas (1225-74). Three periods of Scholasticism are commonly distinguished: medieval period from St. Anselm to Jean Capreolus (1060-1440); Counter-Reformation or the Spanish-Portuguese Revival (1520-1640), declining after the rise of Protestantism and the spread of Cartesianism; and Neo-Scholasticism, officially recognized by Pope Leo XIII in 1879, beginning in the latter half of the nineteenth century to the present time. (Etym. **Latin** *schola*, place of learning, school; from **Greek** *schole*, school; discussion; rest, leisure, employment of leisure time.)

BIBLIOGRAPHY

1. **Aquinas, Thomas, St.,** *Summa Contra Gentiles*, Vol. 1,2,3, Notre Dame, London, 1975

2. " ", *Summa Theologica*, Vol.1, Christian Classics, Allen, Texas, 1984

3. **Augustine, St.,** *The City of God*, Vol.1, Everyman's library; Dent, New York, 1947

4. " ", *Enchiridion on Faith, Hope and Love*, Gateway, Washington D.C, 1992

5. " ", *On Free Choice of the Will*, Hackett Publ., Indianapolis, 1993

6. " ", *Confessions,* Sheed & Ward, New York, 1942

7. **Behe, Michael,** *Science & Evidence for Design in the Universe,* Ignatius, San Francisco, 2002

8. "   ", *Darwin's Black Box,* The Free Press, New York, 1996

9. **Benignus, F.S.C, Br,,** *Nature, Knowledge and God,* Bruce, Milwaukee, 1953

10. **Boethius,** *The Consolation of Philosophy,* Penguin Classics, Markam, Ont., Canada, 1959

11. **Bonaventure St.,** *Breviloquium,* Desclee, Paris, Tournai, Rome, New York, 1963

12. **Brosnan, William, S.J.,** *God and Reason,* Fordham, New York, 1924

13. **Cavanaugh, Joseph, C.S.C.,** *Evidence for our Faith,* Notre Dame, Indiana, 1952

14. **Chesterton, G.K,** *Orthodoxy,* Image, New York, 1959

15. "   ", *What's Wrong With The World,* Sheed

& Ward, New York, 1956

16. "   ", Collected works: *The Illustrated London News*; 1926-1928, Ignatius Press, 1991

17. "   ", *The Outline of Sanity*, Dodd, Mead&Co., New York, 1927

18. **Conway, Rev. Bertrand,** *The Question Box,* Paulist, New York, 1929

19. **Copleston, F, S.J,** *A History of Philosophy* Vol.2, Newman, Westminster, 1950

20. **D'Arcy, M.C,** *The Providence of God and the Problem of Evil*

21. **Dubray, Charles, S.M,** *Introduction to Philosophy*, Longmans & Green, New York, 1928

22. **Doyle, Francis, S.J,** *The Defense of The Catholic Church*, Benzinger,1926

23. **Donlan, T., Murphy, W., Reidy J., Cunningham, F., all O.P.,** *God and His Creation*, 1958

24. **Faber, Fr. Frederick William,** *At the Foot of the Cross, Tan, Illinois, 1978*

25. **Garrigou-Lagrange, R., O.P,** *The Trinity and God the Creator*, Herder, 1952

26. "   ", *Reality*, Herder, St. Louis, 1950

27. "   ", *The One God,* Herder, St. Louis, 1943

28. "   ", *Providence,* Herder, St. Louis, 1946

29. **Gilson, Etienne,** *The Christian Philosophy of St. Augustine*, Octogon Books, 1988

30. **Glenn, Paul, Msgr.,** *Apologetics*, Herder, 1931

31. **Hardon, John, S.J.,** *Modern Catholic Dictionary,* Eternal Life, Kentucky, 2001

32. **Hahn, Scott,** *Where is God in a Ungodly World?*, St. Joseph Communications

33. **Hawkins, D.B**, *The Essentials of Theism*, Sheed & Ward, New York, 1950

34. **John Paul II, Pope,** *Salvifici Doloris*, Apostolic Letter, Pauline, 1984

35. **Kreeft, Peter,** *Making sense out of suffering*, Servant Books, Michigan, 1986

36. "   ", *The Summa of the Summa*, Ignatius, San Francisco, 1990

37. **Lear, Jonathan,** *Aristotle-The Desire to Understand*, Cambridge, 1988

38. **Lewis, C. S,** *The Problem of Pain*, Collier Books, New York, 1962

39. **L'Osservatore Romano,** N. 7, 18 February 2004

40. **McCormick, John, S.J,** *Natural Theology*, Loyola, Chicago, 1943

41. **O'Connor, John, Cardinal & Wiesel, Elie,** *A Journey of Faith*, Primus, New York, 1990

42. **Pohle, Rev. Joseph,** *God, The Author of Nature and The Supernatural,* Herder, St. Louis,1927

43. **Pascal, Blaise,** *Pensees,* Britannica Great Books, Vol.33, 1952

44. **Sharpe, A. B,** *Evil,* Catholic Encyclopedia, Vol.5, R. Appleton, 1909

45. **Schmidt, Austin, S.J.,** *Faith and Reason,* Loyola, Chicago, 1943

46. **Smith, Gerard, S.J,** *Natural Theology,* Macmillan, New York, 1951

47. **Stoddard, John,** *Rebuilding A Lost Faith,* Tan, Illinois, 1990

48. **Stravinskas, Rev. Peter,** *Catholic Dictionary,* Our Sunday Visitor, Indiana, 1993

49. **Wuellner, Bernard, S.J.,** *Dictionary of Scholastic Philosophy,* Bruce, Milwaukee, 1956